Family Connections

PEARSON EARLY LEARNING
Pearson Learning Group

The following people have contributed to the development of this product:

Art and Design: Dorothea Fox, Evelyn O'Shea, Jennifer Visco

Editorial: Carlos Byfield, Teri Crawford Jones, Deborah Eaton, Susan Poskanzer

Inventory: Levon Carter, Jeff Hoitsma

Marketing: Diane Bradley, Laura Egan

Production/Manufacturing: Irene Belinsky, Karen Edmonds, Cheryl Golding, Jennifer McCormack, Cathy Pawlowski, Cindy Talocci

Publishing Operations: Carolyn Coyle, Richetta Lobban

ISBN 1-57212-805-4
Printed in the United States of America
14 15 V036 16 15

Opening the World of Learning™ is a trademark of Pearson Education, Inc.

Pearson
Early
Learning
Pearson Learning Group

1-800-321-3106
www.pearsonlearning.com
www.pearsonearlylearning.com

Table of Contents

Children in preschool programs do better when their parents or caregivers know what is happening in the classroom. Well-informed parents understand how to support children's learning at home. So the goal of this book is to help teachers communicate with families.

The materials in *Family Connections* will help you communicate with parents and caregivers. For each unit in the *Opening the World of Learning* curriculum, there are family letters, home activities, and workshop ideas. There are also many practical suggestions for things parents can do at home. In these pages you will find information sheets on

- reading aloud to young children;

- supporting math learning at home; and

- choosing books for preschoolers.

Opening the World of Learning Family Connections also includes over 100 simple home activities. Each activity supports classroom learning. The activities are easy to do. They require no special materials. Letters to parents also make it simple to share the activity ideas with families.

The workshop ideas in this book are a great way to exchange information. They can also help teachers build good relationships with children's families. There are six workshops, one for each OWL unit. They are designed to help teachers deepen families' understanding of how they can support their children's learning.

The workshop topics have been chosen to reinforce the skills taught in your classroom. They cover reading, math learning at home, oral language, social skills, writing, and environmental print. Because it's important to be responsive to families' concerns as well, you may want to invite questions and suggestions for workshops from caregivers. Then you can create a new workshop, or you can devote part of each workshop to those issues.

The goal of this book is to help families and teachers work together as a team. When that happens, children are more likely to make great strides in learning.

When parents are involved in their children's learning, children have a better chance of succeeding in school. Families who have a strong relationship with teachers know what is happening in their children's classrooms and are more likely to make learning part of their life at home. For this reason, OWL teachers will want to form strong relationships with parents.

It's not always easy for teachers and families to connect. Teachers and the adults in children's families typically are busy. Some parents may not get involved because they do not realize how important they are to their children's learning. Some may be hesitant because of their limited English skills. Others may have had difficulties in school themselves. They may feel shy or uncomfortable around teachers. However, parents care deeply about their children. They will participate if they are invited and shown how to support their children's learning.

There are many ways to keep parents informed and involved. Parent conferences are important. Some teachers also send home activity folders, event calendars, and newsletters. Some sponsor "read-ins" and other enjoyable activities. Others build a corps of parent volunteers. This book provides parent letters, home activities, and workshops to get you started.

All these strategies are good ones. Just as important is a commitment to building a partnership with families. This means that teachers need to acknowledge that parents have important contributions to make—to their children's learning, to the classroom, and to the school community. Families respond when teachers respect their efforts to support their children, whatever the family structure, background, ethnicity, or culture.

Each teacher will find his or her own approach to connecting with families. The goal, however, is always the same—teaming up to help children reach their potential.

Questions to Ask Yourself About Your Communication With Families

- Does my communication include helpful information?
- Am I clear and straightforward?
- Do I explain what I expect children to learn?
- Do I explain my expectations for parents' support?
- Do I ask for information from parents?
- Do I listen carefully?
- Do I respect families' privacy?
- Do I always follow up on parents' questions and seriously consider their suggestions?

Reading at Home

Dear Parents and Caregivers,

The people who study how children learn to read agree: Reading at home is very important—just as important as reading at school! The earlier home reading begins, the better. So this year, we are asking all our parents to read to their children as often as they can. We hope you can read to your child every day.

We expect you will enjoy reading with your child at home as much as we do at school, and we want to support you. The information that follows should help you get started. If you have any questions, please let me know.

_____

Your child's teacher

Why?

Children whose families read to them when they are young do better in school. They know about books and words and letters and sounds. They have experience following a story. They like reading! Early experience with books makes it easier for children to learn to read themselves.

What you do now with your preschooler can make a world of difference. Young children who are read to at home have an easier time learning to read in first grade. Children who are not read to are more likely to struggle with reading, and once a child falls behind, it's hard to catch up.

When?

Plan to read at the same time each day. Make it part of your family's routine. Many families read a book at bedtime. If that is not a good time for you, find another time that works.

We know families are busy. Remember, even just 20 minutes a day can make a difference.

Good reading skills open doors to

- success in school
- better understanding of the world
- positive feelings about yourself as a learner

Where?

Sit side-by-side on your child's bed, a couch, or the floor. Look at the pictures together and let your child help turn the pages. Pack a book for reading on bus rides, trips to Grandma's house, or in the doctor's waiting room.

What?

There are so many great books for children! The local library should have a good selection. Try different kinds of books. Read stories, rhymes, and information books. Notice which kinds of reading your child enjoys most and ask your librarian to help you find more. It's okay to read the same book over and over, too!

You do not have to read in English. It's fine to read books in your first language. Children learn about language from those readings, too. It won't slow down their English learning. In fact, it will help!

How?

You may be surprised at the most important rule for reading to your child:

Have a good time!

Read-aloud time is not a chore for your child to complete. It's a special activity to enjoy together. Most children love hearing stories.

Children who like being read to really want to learn to read. Attitude counts! Show by your own attitude that you think books are interesting and fun. Get cozy, relax, and enjoy the books yourself.

What to Do During a Read-Aloud

As you read, talk with your child about the book. Answer questions and ask questions of your own. This is how your child will learn.

- Name anything your child points to in the pictures.
- Point to pictures yourself and explain things as you read.
- Run your finger under some words as you read them, especially if they are in big, bold print or are fun to say.
- Explain any word your child may not understand.
- Encourage questions and comments—get a conversation going!

Lectura en el hogar

Estimados padres de familia o encargados,

Las personas que estudian cómo aprenden los niños a leer, concuerdan que: la lectura en el hogar es muy importante—¡tan importante como el leer en la escuela! Entre más temprano se comience la lectura en el hogar, mejor. Así que este año, pedimos a todos nuestros padres de familia que les lean a sus hijos tan a menudo como puedan. Esperamos que puedan leerles a sus hijos cada día.

Esperamos que disfruten leer con sus hijos en su hogar tanto como disfrutamos nosotros hacerlo en la escuela, y les ofrecemos nuestro apoyo. La información a continuación les ayudará a comenzar. Favor de comunicarse conmigo si tiene alguna pregunta.

_____

El/la maestro/a de su hijo/a

¿Por qué?

Los niños cuyas familias les leen a temprana edad, progresan más en la escuela.

Ellos saben acerca de los libros, palabras, letras y sonidos. Ellos saben por experiencia la secuencia de una historia. ¡Y les gusta leer! Las experiencias tempranas con los libros logran facilitar que los niños lean por sí mismos.

Lo que usted hace ahora con su hijo/a preescolar puede hacer un mundo de diferencia. Los niños a quienes se les lee en el hogar aprenden a leer con más facilidad en el primer grado. Los niños a quienes no se les lee, son más propensos a tener dificultades con la lectura. Una vez que el/la niño/a se atrase, es más difícil ponerlo/a al día.

¿Cuándo?

Planee leer a la misma hora cada día. Hágalo parte de la rutina de su familia. Muchas familias leen un libro a la hora de acostarse. Si ésta no es una buena hora para usted, encuentre otra hora que le sea más conveniente.

Sabemos que las familias pasan ocupadas. Para asegurarse que alguien le lee a su niño/a preescolar diariamente, tal vez los adultos e hijos mayores de la familia puedan tomar turnos para leer.

Las buenas destrezas de lectura abren las puertas:

- al éxito en la escuela
- a la mejor comprensión del mundo
- a los sentimientos positivos de sí mismo como estudiante.

¿Dónde?

Siéntese al lado de la cama, el sofá o en el piso con su hijo/a, observen los grabados juntos y permita que su hijo/a dé vuelta las páginas. Incluya un libro para leer en viajes en autobús, viajes a la casa de abuelita o en la sala de espera del doctor.

¿Qué?

¡Existen tantos libros excelentes para niños! Es muy probable que la biblioteca local tenga una buena selección. Intente leer diferentes libros. Lea cuentos, rimas y libros de información. Fíjese en el tipo de libro que más le gusta a su hijo/a y pídale a su bibliotecario/a que le ayude a encontrar otros del mismo tipo. ¡Además, está bien leer el mismo libro una y otra vez!

No tiene que leer en inglés. Está bien leer libros en su lengua materna. Los niños también aprenden cosas acerca del lenguaje por medio de estas lecturas. No atrasará su aprendizaje del inglés. ¡Es más, ayudará!

¿Cómo?

Tal vez le sorprenda la regla más importante acerca de leerle a su hijo/a:

¡Disfrútelo!

La hora de lectura en voz alta no es tarea para ser completada por su hijo. Es una actividad especial que deben disfrutar juntos. A la mayoría de los niños les encanta escuchar cuentos.

Los niños quienes disfrutan que les lean, realmente desean aprender a leer. ¡La actitud cuenta! Muestre con su propia actitud que usted cree que los libros son interesantes y divertidos. Acomódese, relájese, y disfrute usted también de los libros.

Lo que se hace durante la lectura oral (en voz alta)

Mientras lee, platique con su hijo/a acerca del libro. Conteste preguntas y haga usted algunas. Así es como su niño aprenderá.

- Nombre lo que su hijo señale en los grabados o ilustraciones.
- Señale usted grabados también y explique mientras lee.
- Pase los dedos debajo de algunas palabras mientras las lee, especialmente si están en letra impresa grande, en negrita, o sean divertidas para pronunciar.
- Explique cualquier palabra que el niño no entienda.
- Anímelo/a a hacer preguntas y comentarios—¡estimule la conversación!

Books to Read With Your Child

A Note to Family Members: The most important thing about choosing books to read with your child is to find books you both enjoy. Read lots of different kinds of books. Notice which ones your child wants to read again. Don't be shy about asking for advice at the local library. Librarians often love to help parents find books their preschoolers will like. Just to get you started, here are some great books that relate to topics we'll be exploring at school.

Unit 1: Family

Abuela by Arthur Dorros
A girl and her grandmother fly all over New York City, enjoying city scenes and each other.

A Birthday Basket for Tía/Una canasta de cumpleaños para Tía by Pat Mora
A young girl makes a special birthday surprise for her 90-year-old great aunt.

Brothers & Sisters by Ellen B. Senisi
This book explores brother-sister relationships with beautiful photographs.

A Chair for My Mother/Un sillón para mi mamá by Vera B. Williams
A young girl and her mother and grandmother save all their coins to buy a big, soft armchair.

Julius, the Baby of the World/Julius, el rey de la casa by Kevin Henkes
A jealous older sister discovers her loyalty to her baby brother.

The Tale of Peter Rabbit/El cuento de Pedrito Conejo by Beatrix Potter
Peter has an adventure and is glad to return to his family.

Unit 2: Friends

Chicka Chicka Boom Boom by Bill Martin Jr.
In this ABC tale, lively letters meet at the top of a coconut tree.

Four Friends in Autumn by Tomie de Paola
Mistress Pig makes dinner for her friends. But where did all the food go?

Kipper's A to Z: An Alphabet Adventure by Mick Inkpen
Two friends have a day of fun in this ABC book.

The Leaving Morning/La mañana de la despedida by Angela Johnson
A brother and sister say good-bye to all their neighborhood friends and family, as they get ready to move.

Where the Wild Things Are/Donde viven los monstruos by Maurice Sendak
Sent to bed for being naughty, a little boy makes some unusual friends.

Unit 3: Wind and Water

The Desert is My Mother/El desierto es mi madre by Pat Mora
This bilingual book tells a story of the desert, with its warm winds, sudden thunderstorms, and more.

Jimmy's Boa and the Big Splash Birthday Bash by Trinka H. Noble
Meggie returns home from Jimmy's birthday party soaking wet, and her explanation is wild!

Raindrop, Plop! by Wendy Cheyette Lewison
Counting raindrops until the sun comes out is fun!

Rata Pata Scata Fata by Phillis Gershator
In this story from the Caribbean, a boy makes many wishes, including a wish for rain.

Swimmy/Nadarin by Leo Lionni
Deep in the ocean, little Swimmy learns how to escape all the big fish.

The Wind Blew by Pat Hutchins
The wind snatches things and mixes them up before blowing out to sea.

Books to Read With Your Child

A Color of His Own by Leo Lionni
Everything has a color all its own except the little chameleon.

How Is a Crayon Made?/¿Cómo se hace un crayón? by Oz Charles
Come join a tour of the Crayola™ crayon factory.

I Went Walking/Salí de paseo by Sue Williams
A child goes out for a walk, sees animals of many colors, and has a wonderful time.

Mouse Paint/Pinta ratones by Ellen Stoll Walsh
Three white mice dip themselves in paint and play with colors.

New Shoes for Silvia/Zapatos nuevos para Silvia by Johanna Hurwitz
Silvia receives a present from her aunt—wonderful bright red shoes.

Where Is the Green Sheep? by Mem Fox
All kinds and colors of sheep show up in this rhyming book, but where is the green sheep?

Bedtime for Frances/La hora de acorstarse de Francisca by Russell Hoban
Frances delays her bedtime and worries about scary things in the dark.

Goodnight Moon/Buenas noches, luna by Margaret Wise Brown
This bedtime classic has lovely shadows and reflections.

Kitten's First Full Moon by Kevin Henkes
Kitten sees a full moon and thinks it's a bowl of milk.

Oh, Look! by Patricia Polacco
Three goats see lots of exciting things, including their own reflections in a fun house mirror.

Snowmen at Night by Caralyn Buehner
What do snowmen do at night? They play in the shadows until it gets light.

This Little Light of Mine illustrated by Reg Sandland
This African American spiritual from slavery times tells about the light inside all of us.

As Big as You by Elaine Greenstein
A mother compares her growing baby to the sizes of things in nature.

The Carrot Seed/ La semilla de zanahoria by Ruth Krauss
No matter what anyone says, a little boy is sure the carrot seed he planted will grow.

Kids Pick the Funniest Poems by Bruce Lansky
The laughs will just grow bigger and bigger as you read these funny poems.

Leo, the Late Bloomer/Leo, el retoño tardío by Robert Kraus
Leo is a little tiger who learns everything at his own pace, and that's okay!

Spring/Primavera by Ron Hirschi.
All kinds of wonderful plants and animals grow in the spring!

Watch Me Grow: Bear by Lisa Magloff
This close-up look at a growing bear is part of a series of "Watch Me Grow" books, all with great color photos.

Math at Home

Dear Parents and Caregivers,

Many activities we're doing this year will prepare your child for success in math in kindergarten and first grade. These pages tell how you can help at home.

To help your child learn about math, point out numbers, sizes, and shapes, and count items with your child whenever you have the chance. The following ideas can help you support your child's learning. But here's the most important thing: Enjoy math with your child! Let me know if you have any questions,

_____

Your child's teacher

Why?

Young children who already have a lot of experiences in math have a better chance of succeeding in math in school. It's that simple. Sorting and counting objects and talking about shapes and numbers can make a very big difference for your child.

What?

What is "math" at this age? It's counting, comparing things, and solving simple problems in everyday life. Most children enjoy games, and a lot of math can be learned by playing games.

When children play, they often use mathematics.

- They count. ("She has three blocks and I only have one.")
- They share. ("Here's a car for you and a car for me.")
- They solve problems. ("You go first, then me, then John.")
- They notice sizes and shapes. ("It's in the big, square box.")

Simple toys and objects like kitchen utensils, crayons, and paper and pencil are all tools that can help your child learn math skills. Here are some things your preschooler can learn about mathematics with your support and help.

- Recognizing and naming shapes and numbers
- Counting
- Learning how to write some numbers
- Using math language, like *more* and *less*, *taller* and *shorter*, *lighter* and *heavier*, and *half of*
- Sorting objects into groups

When, Where, and How?

The key is to weave activities into your daily routine. Here are a few activity ideas that don't require much extra time . . . just a little effort.

- Go for a walk and count the number of red cars or trucks you see. Observe and talk about what makes them different.

- As you use items at home, such as mixing bowls or towels, comment to your child about their sizes. Use words like *small*, *medium*, and *large*, *bigger* and *smaller*, *lighter* and *heavier*.

- Give your child some items of different sizes to arrange—sets of measuring spoons or plastic mixing bowls will work. Also let your child help you sort and fold towels and washcloths from the laundry.

- While grocery shopping, note the aisle numbers you visit and count the number of people in line ahead of you at the register.

- Play with numbered refrigerator magnets and name them. Find things to match to the numbers: one nose, two eyes, five fingers on one hand.

- Show your child your telephone number. Help your child match your telephone number by arranging magnetic refrigerator numbers or numbers you write on small squares of paper.

- Use a calendar to mark off days. Count the days or weeks until a special event, like a birthday or holiday.

- When removing spoons, forks, and table knives from the dish drying rack or the dishwasher, put them on the table for your child to sort for putting away.

- Help your child line up measuring cups by size. Let your child play with these in the tub at bath time, or provide a tub of water on the kitchen table for play with these items.

- Write numbers with a pencil as your child watches, and talk about the lines as you make them. Then let your child try.

Tip #1 Keep it positive! Show an interest in numbers and shapes, and your child will too. Praise your child for effort made.

Tip #2 Don't push! Never drill your child or put him or her on the spot for answers. Provide information and play along to show your child how.

Tip #3 Talk about it! As your child plays, observe what he or she is doing and talk about it. Answer questions or ask some of your own and you will both learn.

Tip #4 Follow your child's lead! If your child loses interest in doing something you suggest, stop for now or try something else.

Matemáticas en el hogar

Estimados padres de familia o encargados,

Muchas de las actividades que hacemos este año prepararán a su hijo para tener éxito en matemáticas en kínder y primer grado. Estas páginas le cuentan cómo puede ayudar usted en su hogar.

Para ayudarles a sus hijos a aprender matemáticas, señale números, tamaños y figuras, y cuente artículos con su hijo/a cuando tenga la oportunidad. Las ideas a continuación pueden ayudarle a brindar a su hijo/a apoyo en el aprendizaje. Pero esto es lo más importante: ¡Disfrute las matemáticas con su hijo!

Favor de comunicarse conmigo si tiene alguna pregunta.

_____

El/la maestro/a de su hijo/a

¿Por qué?

Los niños jóvenes que ya han tenido mucha experiencia con las matemáticas tienen mejor oportunidad de lograr éxito en la escuela en esta materia. Es así de simple. Clasificar y contar objetos y hablar de las figuras y números puede representar una gran diferencia para su hijo/a.

¿Qué?

¿Qué son las matemáticas a esta edad? Es contar, comparar cosas y resolver problemas simples de la vida diaria. La mayoría de los niños disfrutan los juegos, y muchas cosas de las matemáticas se aprenden jugando.

Cuando los niños juegan, ellos usan a menudo las matemáticas.

- Ellos cuentan. ("Ella tiene tres bloques y tengo sólo uno".)

- Ellos comparten. ("Aquí hay un carro para mí y otro para ti".)

- Ellos resuelven problemas. ("Tú vas primero, luego yo y después Juan".)

- Ellos observan tamaños y figuras o formas. ("Está detrás de la caja grande y cuadrada".)

Juguetes sencillos y objetos como utensilios de cocina, crayones y papel y lapiz son herramientas que ayudarán a su hijo/a a aprender destrezas básicas de matemáticas. Aquí hay algunas cosas que su niño/a preescolar puede aprender acerca las matemáticas cuando usted le brinda su apoyo.

- Reconocer y nombrar figuras y números

- Contar

- Aprender a escribir algunos números

- Usar lenguaje de matemáticas, tal como *más* y *menos, más alto* y *más bajo, más liviano* y *más pesado* y *la mitad de*

- Clasificar objetos en grupos

¿Cuándo, dónde, y cómo?

La clave es combinar las actividades con su rutina diaria. Aquí hay algunas actividades que no requieren mucho tiempo adicional . . . sólo un poco de esfuerzo.

- Tomen una caminata y cuenten el número de carros rojos que ustedes ven. Observen y platiquen acerca de qué los hace diferentes.

- Cuando use artículos en el hogar, tales como tazas de mezclar y toallas, coméntele a su hijo/a acerca de los tamaños. Use palabras como *pequeño*, *mediano*, *grande*, *más grande* y *más pequeño*, *más liviano* y *más pesado*.

- Permita que su hijo/a ordene cosas de diferentes tamaños—juegos de cucharas de medir o tazas plásticas para mezclar. También permita que su hijo/a le ayude a seleccionar y doblar toallas y paños del lavado.

- Mientras anda de compras en el supermercado, anote los números de las hileras que visita y cuente el número de personas que estén en la fila delante de usted en la caja.

- Juegue con imanes de refrigeradora numerados y nómbrelos. Busque cosas que se puedan parear con los números: una naríz, dos ojos, cinco dedos de una mano.

- Muéstrele a su hijo/a su número de teléfono. Ayúdele a su hijo/a a ordenar los imanes numerados en el mismo orden de su número telefónico o de números que usted puede escribir en trocitos cuadrados de papel.

- Use un calendario para marcar los días. Cuente los días o semanas que faltan para la celebración de un acontecimiento especial, como un cumpleaños o día festivo.

- Cuando esté sacando cucharas, tenedores y cuchillos de mesa de la lavadora de platos o de la rejilla para secar platos, colóquelos sobre la mesa para que su hijo/a los pueda clasificar o guardar.

- Ayúdele a su hijo/a alinear tazas de medir por tamaño. Permita que su hijo/a juegue con éstas en la tina a la hora del baño, o coloque una tina con agua sobre la mesa de la cocina para que juegue con estos artículos.

- Escriba números con un lápiz mientras su hijo/a observa, y platique acerca de las líneas mientras las hace. Luego haga que su hijo/a lo intente.

Consejo #1 ¡Sea positivo! Muestre su interés en los números y figuras o formas, y su hijo/a hará lo mismo. Elogie a su hijo por el esfuerzo hecho.

Consejo #2 ¡No presione! Nunca apresure ni presione a su hijo/a para que responda de inmediato. Provea información y disimule para mostrarle a su hijo/a cómo contestar.

Consejo #3 ¡Platique sobre el asunto! Observe lo que su hijo hace mientras juega y platique acerca de esto. Conteste preguntas o haga usted algunas y ambos aprenderán.

Consejo #4 ¡Siga la dirección que toma su hijo/a! Si su hijo/a pierde interés en hacer algo que usted sugiere, deténgase por el momento y trate otra cosa.

Date:

Dear Family,
We're reading books and talking about families at school. We hope you'll take some time to talk about families at home, too.

The activities on the next page are things you can do to help your child learn. We hope you can complete at least ___ of the activities. Do them in any order. Circle the ones you complete. Then bring the page back to school.

Have fun!

Thank you,

_____

Your child's teacher

Books we are reading at school

- *Whistle for Willie* by Ezra Jack Keats
- *Oonga Boonga* by Frieda Wishinsky
- *Noisy Nora* by Rosemary Wells
- *Peter's Chair* by Ezra Jack Keats
- *Corduroy* by Don Freeman
- *Time for Bed* by Mem Fox
- *Let's Make Music* by Margaret Clyne and Rachel Griffiths
- *Over in the Meadow* by Ezra Jack Keats

Unidad 1

Fecha:

Estimada familia,

Estamos leyendo libros y platicando sobre familias en nuestra clase. Esperamos que ustedes también tomen tiempo en su hogar para hablar acerca de familias.

Las actividades en la próxima página son las que pueden ayudar a su hijo/a a aprender. Esperamos que puedan completar por lo menos ___ de las actividades. Complétenlas en cualquier orden. Circulen las que hayan completado. Luego envíen la página de regreso a la escuela.

¡Diviértanse!

Gracias,

_____

El/la maestro/a de su hijo/a

Libros que leemos en inglés en la escuela

- *Whistle for Willie* by Ezra Jack Keats
- *Oonga Boonga* by Frieda Wishinsky
- *Noisy Nora* by Rosemary Wells
- *Peter's Chair* by Ezra Jack Keats
- *Corduroy* by Don Freeman
- *Time for Bed* by Mem Fox
- *Let's Make Music* by Margaret Clyne and Rachel Griffiths
- *Over in the Meadow* by Ezra Jack Keats

Unit 1
Activities For You And Your Child

Let your child help set the table. Talk about shapes and colors.

Show your child his or her baby pictures. Talk about them together.

Ask your child to help you make a sandwich for lunch. Talk about each step.

Have a scavenger hunt in your home. Find things that can grow, stretch, or make noise.

Help your child write his or her name. Decorate it and hang it on the door of your child's room.

Tell your child about something that happened when you were little.

Count the people in your family. Use your fingers to keep a tally as you count.

Look at family pictures together. Talk about the people in your family.

Call a family member. Say the numbers and point to them on the phone. Let your child press them.

Sing the Alphabet Song together.

Read a book. Point to things in the pictures as you read about them in the story.

Turn off the car radio and talk with your child as you drive.

Measure your child by taping a strip of paper to the wall and marking it over time.

Keep a list called "Things I Can Do By Myself." Let your child decide what to add to the list day by day.

Take your child to the library. Choose books to read together.

Play house. Let your child decide who is the baby and who is the mommy or daddy.

If there's a baby in your family, name baby items as you shop. Talk about what babies need.

Trace your child's hands and label the drawing with his or her name. Then let your child trace your hands.

Please return this sheet by _____. Child_____ Parent _____
                                  (date)   (name)   (name)

Comments? We'd love to hear from you._____

_____

Unidad 1
Actividades para usted y su hijo/a

Nuestro tema del mes es:
"La familia"

Pensamiento del mes:
¡Diviértanse! Escoja las actividades que usted y su hijo vayan a disfrutar más.

Muéstrele a su hijo/a sus fotos de bebé. Hable acerca de éstas.

Miren las fotos de la familia juntos. Hable usted acerca de las personas en su familia.

Platique con su hijo/a con respecto a algo que le sucedió a usted cuando usted era niño/a.

Canten la canción del abecedario juntos

Pídale a su hijo/a que haga una torta para el almuerzo. Hable acerca de cada paso.

Permita que su hijo/a ponga la mesa. Hable acerca de figuras y colores.

Llame a un miembro de la familia. Diga los números del teléfono y señale éstos en el mismo teléfono. Permita que su hijo/a oprima las teclas.

Ayúdele a su hijo/a a escribir su propio nombre. Decore el nombre y colóquelo en la puerta de la habitación de él/ella.

Lleven a cabo una búsqueda de objetos en su hogar. Busque cosas que crecen, estiran, o que hagan ruido.

Cuente el número de personas en su familia. Use sus dedos para contar y llevar la cuenta.

Mantenga una lista titulada "Cosas que puedo hacer por mi cuenta". Permita que su hijo/a decida qué agregar a la lista diariamente.

Mida el crecimiento de su hijo/a sobre una tira de papel colocada en la pared y marque el crecimiento a medida que pasa el tiempo.

Apague el radio de su auto y platique con su hijo/a mientras maneja.

Lleve a su hijo/a a la biblioteca. Escojan libros para leer juntos.

Lean un libro. Señale cosas de los grabados o ilustraciones mientras leen acerca de los mismos en el cuento.

Trace las manos de su hijo/a y ponga su nombre dentro del dibujo de las manos para identificarlas. Entonces, que su hijo/a haga lo mismo con las manos suyas.

Jueguen de casita. Permita que su hijo/a decida quién es el bebé, la mamá o el papá.

Si hay un bebé en la familia, nombre los artículos de bebé cuando los compre. Platique acerca de lo que un bebé necesita.

Favor de devolver esta hoja a más tardar _____. _____ del niño/de la niña _____del padre de familia
(fecha)   (nombre)   (nombre)

¿Comentarios? Nos encantaría tener noticias de usted. _____

Unit 1 Workshop: Reading with Your Child

This workshop will:
- introduce family members to the content of Unit 1;
- explain the importance of reading at home;
- provide parents with the information about reading effectively to their children.

Suggested Warm-up Activity

Have name tags ready for parents to fill out with their first names. To begin to create a sense of community, organize parents into groups of three or four. Ask them to introduce themselves and tell their children's names and ages.

Workshop Suggestions

1. Convey the importance of reading at home. Start by saying that children who are often read to at this age have a much higher chance of becoming successful readers—not just in first grade, but throughout their school years! Explain that family help is needed. Although you read to children every day and talk with them about books, you cannot give each child the personal attention a parent or caregiver can provide at home.

2. Demonstrate a read-aloud. Choose a book you especially enjoy. Model pointing to pictures, making meaningful asides, and asking what will happen next. Ask questions that a listening child might ask, then respond as a parent might. Practice! Don't wing it.

3. Discuss the read-aloud techniques you used. Explain how talking with children about books enriches the experience and builds reading and language skills. You may want to refer to a checklist of important points to include, but do not overload parents with academic details.

4. Invite questions.

Unit 1

Introduce the theme of Unit 1: Family. Give a quick overview of the books and a few activities. Encourage parents to explore the theme at home as well, explaining family relationships; looking at family photos; talking about siblings and sharing parents' attention; and discussing how family members have fun together and help one another.

Closing the Workshop

Hand out "Reading at Home" (pages 6–9) and the suggested list of reading books for Units 1 to 3 (page 10). Encourage parents to read to their children every day. Explain how your lending library will work, if you have one.

> Be very warm and welcoming. Say hello to each parent and address each one by name. Move around and talk with all family members, not just those you already know.

> **Keep in Mind...**
>
> Emphasize the value of reading to children and helping children become good readers, without diminishing the dignity of family members who may not read very much or very well themselves.

Unit 2

Date:

Dear Family,

We're reading books and talking about friends at school. We hope you'll take some time to talk about friends at home, too.

The activities on the next page are things you can do to help your child learn. We hope you can complete at least ___ of the activities. Do them in any order. Circle the ones you complete. Then bring the page back to school.

Have fun!

Thank you,

_____

Your child's teacher

Books we are reading at school

- *Dandelion* by Don Freeman
- *Hooray, a Piñata!* by Elisa Kleven
- *A Letter for Amy* by Ezra Jack Keats
- *Matthew and Tilly* by Rebecca Jones
- *The Little Red Hen (Makes a Pizza)* by Philemon Sturges
- *Golden Bear* by Ruth Young
- *Hush!* by Mingfong Ho
- *Road Builders* by B.G. Hennessy

Fecha:

Estimada familia,

Estamos leyendo libros y platicando acerca de los amigos en la escuela. Esperamos que ustedes también tomen tiempo en su hogar para platicar acerca de los amigos.

Las actividades sugeridas en la próxima página son las que pueden llevar a cabo para ayudarle a su hijo/a a aprender. Esperamos que puedan completar por lo menos ___ de las actividades. Las pueden completar en cualquier orden. Circule las que completen. Luego envíe la página de regreso a la escuela.

¡Diviértanse!

Gracias,

_____

El/la maestro/a de su hijo/a

Libros que leemos en inglés en la escuela

- *Dandelion* by Don Freeman
- *Hooray, a Piñata!* by Elisa Kleven
- *A Letter for Amy* by Ezra Jack Keats
- *Matthew and Tilly* by Rebecca Jones
- *The Little Red Hen (Makes a Pizza)* by Philemon Sturges
- *Golden Bear* by Ruth Young
- *Hush!* by Mingfong Ho
- *Road Builders* by B.G. Hennessy

Unit 2
Activities For You And Your Child

Tell your child about things you did for fun with your best friend as a child.

Have a scavenger hunt in your home for things that are sticky, smooth, cold, rough, flat, and soft.

Play a simple card game, like Go Fish. Talk about the action as you play. Point out that you're taking turns.

Visit a bakery in a supermarket. Talk about food items and the workers who make them.

Play a song you both like. Drum along on the floor.

Ask your child to think of things that begin with the same sound as his or her name. Write them down, spelling out the letters as you write.

Play "Follow the Leader." Jump, crawl, run, and spin, naming each way to move.

Take your child to the post office. Talk about how letters get where they're going.

Watch an educational TV show. Talk about the action and sing the letter and number songs.

Play a clue game: "I'm thinking of something in the room. It's big and white and cold inside."

Invite your child to draw a picture of a friend. Ask your child to tell you about it.

Make a list of "Things We Like to Do." Post it on the refrigerator and add to it each day.

Let your child help you make a pizza. Name the ingredients, talk about shapes, and count as you put on different toppings.

Read a storybook about friends. Talk with your child about the pictures as you read.

As you drive or ride on the bus, talk about which way you're going and how you know where you will turn.

Let your child help you make a grocery list by checking for items you need. Spell out words as you write: "We need jelly, j-e-l-l-y."

Invite a friend over to play. Beforehand, talk about which toys your child will share.

Together, make a card for a friend. Your child can scribble a message, put on the stamp, and mail it.

Please return this sheet by _____. Child_____ Parent _____
(date)   (name)   (name)

Comments? We'd love to hear from you._____

_____

Unidad 2
Actividades para usted y su hijo/a

Nuestro tema del mes es:
"Los amigos"

Pensamiento del mes: ¡A los niños a quienes se les lee a temprana edad les va mejor en la escuela!

Platique con su hijo/a acerca de cosas que hacía usted con su mejor amigo/a cuando era niño/a.

Visite la reposteria de un supermercado. Platique acerca de los artículos comestibles y de los trabajadores que los preparan.

Vea un programa educativo en la televisión. Platique acerca de la acción y canten la canción de las letras y los números.

Lea un libro de cuentos acerca de amigos. Platique con su hijo/a acerca de los grabados mientras lee.

Lleven a cabo una búsqueda de objetos en la casa y busquen cosas que sean pegajosas, suaves, frías, ásperas, planas y blandas.

Jueguen "Sigan al líder". Brinquen, gateen, corran, y viren, nombrando la dirección que van a seguir.

Invite a su hijo/a a dibujar a un/a amigo/a. Pídale a su hijo/a que le cuente acerca del dibujo.

Invite a un amigo de su hijo/a su casa a jugar. De antemano, hable con su hijo/a acerca de los juguetes que compartirá.

Ponga una canción que les guste a los dos. Lleve el ritmo tocando en el piso.

Lleve a su hijo/a al correo. Platique acerca de la manera que las cartas llegan a su destino.

Permita que su hijo/a le ayude hacer una pizza. Nombre los ingredientes, platique sobre las figuras o formas, y cuente los diferentes aderezos/salsas que se usan.

Hagan juntos una tarjeta para un amigo. Su hijo/a puede escribir un mensaje, colocar la estampilla en el sobre y enviarla.

Jueguen un simple juego de cartas/naipes, tal como "Adivina mi carta". Platique acerca de lo que hace mientras juegan. Señale que cada uno toma turnos.

Juegue un juego de adivinanzas: "Estoy pensando en algo dentro de la habitación. Es grande y blanco y frío por dentro. ¿Qué es?".

Mientras viajen en un autobús, platique sobre la dirección que el autobús va a seguir y cuándo va a virar.

Pídale a su hijo/a que nombre cosas que comienzan con el mismo sonido que el primer sonido de su nombre. Escríbalas, y deletree a la misma vez que escribe.

Haga una lista de "Cosas que nos gusta hacer". Colóquela sobre la refrigeradora y agregue algo cada día.

Permita que su hijo le ayude hacer una lista de compras de artículos que hacen falta en la casa. Deletree las palabras mientras las escribe: "Necesitamos jalea, j-a-l-e-a".

Favor de devolver esta hoja a más tardar _____. _____ del niño/de la niña _____del padre de familia
(fecha)   (nombre)   (nombre)

¿Comentarios? Nos encantaría tener noticias de usted. _____

Unit 2 Workshop: Conversations With Children

This workshop will:
- introduce family members to the content of Unit 2;
- explain the importance of conversations for increasing children's language skills;
- provide parents with models of and suggestions about effective conversations with preschoolers.

Suggested Warm-up Activity

Organize parents into pairs. Have them role-play a parent and child. The "parent" should try to get a conversation going, beginning with, "What did you do at school today?" (Remind those playing the "child" how often preschoolers answer with "nothing," "I don't know," or a shrug.) After three minutes, switch roles.

Workshop Suggestions

1. Invite parents to share any approaches that worked well for getting the "child" to talk. Repeat the exercise yourself, with a parent volunteer playing the child. Follow up with a discussion.

2. Explain that you want children in your class to learn a lot of words, because this will help them learn to read. Confide that the goal of the workshop is to convince participants to go home and talk, talk, talk with their children—during meals, at bedtime, in the car, in the line at the supermarket, and at any time an opportunity arises—because you really need their help to reach the goals you've set for their children this year.

3. Share a few oral language development strategies with parents. (Refer to the OWL teacher's guides.) Rather than telling parents what to do, explain that "this is how we approach it in school."Give specific examples for each one:
   - we try to keep conversations going back and forth
   - we keep it open-ended. We encourage children to "tell what happened" or why or how they did something
   - we avoid over-simplifying, because one goal of our conversations is to stretch children's vocabulary and understanding

4. Invite questions.

Unit 2

Introduce the theme of Unit 2: Friends. Quickly review topics, books, and activities. Encourage parents to discuss the theme at home as well, exploring feelings and observing how friends have fun together, help one another, and sometimes have conflicts.

Closing the Workshop

Reiterate the importance of talking with young children. Distribute a list of language development suggestions. Let parents know that you invite questions and stand ready to help them in any way you can.

> Tell bilingual parents that children can learn two languages at once. It won't harm their English learning. Families can talk in the language they know best.

Keep in Mind...

Convey information about effective conversations with children without in any way challenging participants' parenting styles.

> Most 5-year-olds know about 5,000 words. A few know up to 10,000. However, some know only about 3,000.

Date:

Dear Family,
We're reading books and talking about wind and water at school. We hope you'll take some time to talk about wind and water (and weather!) at home, too.

The activities on the next page are things you can do to help your child learn. We hope you can complete at least ___ of the activities. Do them in any order. Circle the ones you complete. Then bring the page back to school.

Have fun!

Thank you,

_____

Your child's teacher

Books we are reading at school

- *Gilberto and the Wind* by Marie Hall Ets
- *A Hat for Minerva Louise* by Janet M. Stoeke
- *The Snowy Day* by Ezra Jack Keats
- *One Dark Night* by Hazel Hutchins
- *Rabbits and Raindrops* by Jim Arnosky
- *The Very Noisy Night* by Diana Hendry
- *Bringing the Rain to Kapiti Plain* by Verna Aardema
- *See How They Grow: Kitten* by Jane Burton

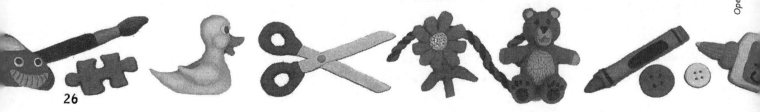

Unidad 3

Fecha:

Estimada familia,

En la escuela estamos leyendo libros que tienen que ver con el viento y el agua. Esperamos que ustedes también tomen tiempo en su hogar para platicar acerca del viento y el agua (y el estado del tiempo).

Las actividades sugeridas en la próxima página son cosas que pueden hacer para ayudarle a su hijo/a a aprender. Esperamos que puedan completar por lo menos ___ de las actividades. Las pueden completar en cualquier orden. Circulen las que completen. Luego envíen la página de regreso a la escuela.

¡Diviértanse!

Gracias,

_____

El/la maestro/a de su hijo/a

Libros que leemos en inglés en la escuela

- *Gilberto and the Wind* by Marie Hall Ets
- *A Hat for Minerva Louise* by Janet M. Stoeke
- *The Snowy Day* by Ezra Jack Keats
- *One Dark Night* by Hazel Hutchins
- *Rabbits and Raindrops* by Jim Arnosky
- *The Very Noisy Night* by Diana Hendry
- *Bringing the Rain to Kapiti Plain* by Verna Aardema
- *See How They Grow: Kitten* by Jane Burton

Theme of the Month:
"Wind and Water"
Thought for the Month:
You are your child's first and most important teacher.

Go outside on a windy day. Notice all the ways you can tell the wind is blowing and talk about them.

At bath time, add toys and plastic cups to the tub. Notice which things sink, float, squirt, or soak up water.

Read a few pages in a new storybook. At an exciting point, ask, "What do you think is going to happen next?" Listen to your child's ideas, then keep reading.

Turn on some music you both like. Dance!

In the tub, float plastic lids. Blow on them and give little plastic animals boat rides. Talk about the wind.

Read signs out loud while riding in the car or bus. Spell the words on them: "That's a stop sign, S-T-O-P."

Take a walk in the rain with your child. Talk about the raindrops and the sounds they make.

Play a rhyming game: "I see something wet and it rhymes with *lane*. It's __ (rain)!" Make the clues easy so the game is fun.

Let your child blow through a straw. See if he or she can find three things in your home that can be moved easily that way.

Each night at bedtime, talk about one way your child was helpful during this day.

Let your child help load and unload the dryer. Talk about how the clothes feel and look when going in and coming out.

Let your child help feed your dog, cat, or pet bird tonight. Talk about what your pet needs to be healthy and happy.

Teach your child a nursery rhyme or street rhyme you said as a child. Then let your child teach one to you.

During a thunderstorm, watch the sky through a window. Talk about what you see. Count slowly between the lightning and the thunder.

Watch the weather forecast. Explain words such as *windy*, *gusts*, or *humidity*. The next day, discuss whether the forecast was correct.

Visit a playground. As your child plays on the equipment, describe the actions: *over*, *under*, *around*, and *through*.

Go on a shape hunt in a magazine or catalog. Find circles, squares, triangles, and rectangles. Help your child trace the shapes with a finger.

Please return this sheet by _____. Child_____ Parent _____
(date)   (name)   (name)

Comments? We'd love to hear from you._____

Unidad 3
Actividades para usted y su hijo/a

Nuestro tema del mes es: "El viento y el agua"

Pensamiento del mes: Usted es el primer y más importante maestro/a de su hijo/a.

Enseñe una rima a su hijo/a o alguna adivinanza que aprendió de niño/a. Luego permita que su hijo le enseñe una.

Pongan música que ambos disfrutan. ¡Bailen!

Salgan a pasear un día ventoso. Observen las direcciones en las que sopla el viento y platiquen acerca de eso.

Permita que su hijo/a sople a través de una paja o pajilla. Vea si él o ella puede hallar tres cosas en su hogar que se puedan mover fácilmente de esa misma manera.

A la hora del baño, incluya juguetes y vasos plásticos en la tina o bañera. Observe los objetos que se hunden, flotan, echan agua o absorben agua.

Durante una tormenta eléctrica, observen el cielo por la ventana. Platiquen acerca de lo que ven. Comiencen a contar lentamente entre relámpagos y truenos.

Vean el pronóstico del tiempo. Explique palabras tales como *ventoso*, *ráfagas* o *humedad*. Al siguiente día comenten si el pronóstico estaba acertado o no.

Permita que su hijo/a alimente a su perro, gato o pájaro esta noche. Platique acerca de lo que su mascota necesita para permanecer sano y estar contento.

Salga a caminar bajo la lluvia con su hijo/a. Platiquen acerca de las gotas de lluvia y los sonidos que hacen.

Lea algunas páginas de un libro de cuentos diferente. Al llegar a un punto emocionante, pregunte, "¿Qué crees que va a suceder después?". Escuche las ideas de su niño, entonces siga leyendo.

Permita que su hijo/a le ayude a llenar y vaciar la secadora de ropa. Platique sobre cómo luce y se siente la ropa antes de ponerla y después de sacarla.

Busquen figuras geométricas en revistas o catálogos. Busquen círculos, cuadrados, triángulos y rectángulos. Ayude a su hijo/a a trazar las figuras con un dedo.

Visiten un patio de recreo o campo de juegos. Pídale a su hijo/a que describa las acciones: sobre, *debajo*, *alrededor* y a *través*, mientras juegan.

Cada noche al acostarse, platique sobre algo útil que su hijo/a haya hecho durante el día.

Compartan un juego de rimás: "Veo algo empapado de agua y rima con *helado*. Está_____(mo -ja-do)". Provea pistas fáciles para que el juego sea divertido.

En la tina, pongan tapas plásticas a flotar. Sople sobre ellas y coloque animalitos plásticos sobre las mismas y lleve los animalitos en un viaje en bote. Platiquen acerca del viento.

Lean rótulos en voz alta mientras viajen en carro o autobús. Deletree las palabras de los rótulos: "Es un alto, A-l-t-o".

Favor de devolver esta hoja a más tardar _____. _____ del niño/de la niña _____del padre de familia
(fecha)   (nombre)   (nombre)

¿Comentarios? Nos encantaría tener noticias de usted. _____

This workshop will:
- introduce family members to the content of Unit 3;
- reinforce family members' understanding of the benefits and techniques of reading aloud to their children;
- give family members an appreciation of the complexity of learning to write and some ideas for helping children develop writing skills.

Suggested Warm-up Activity

Have paper and crayons ready. Organize family members into pairs. Ask them to imagine they are demonstrating letter formation to a child and take turns writing their initials, explaining the process aloud.

Workshop Suggestions

1. Write your own initials on a flip chart, explaining the process aloud as you would to a child, and answering any questions parents have. Show some writing samples from your class. Explain that writing letters typically emerges slowly, with practice, after a lot of experimentation. The first step toward writing is to give children plenty of opportunities to write in their own unique ways.

2. Explain that to become successful writers, children need to know how to combine lines to make letters, how to put letters together to make words, and how to organize their thoughts to figure out what they want to say. Another step is making a connection between different letters and sounds. You may want to present a song or another activity from *Songs, Word Play, Letters,* to show one playful way this information can be conveyed.

3. Present strategies for helping children learn to write, including:
   - providing opportunities to write by making materials like paper, pencils, crayons, markers, junk mail, and envelopes available
   - explaining what you're writing as you write grocery lists, letters, phone messages, and so on
   - helping children write their own names
   - singing songs and playing games that involve letter sounds
   - writing labels that children dictate for their drawings, then reading them aloud

Reassure parents that once children begin to form letters, reversals and writing in incorrect directions is normal for this age.

Unit 3

Introduce the theme of Unit 3: *Wind and Water.* Give a quick overview of topics, books, and activities. Suggest that parents explore the theme at home as well. Encourage them to allow their children to observe and explore, because that's how they will learn most.

Closing the Workshop

Quickly summarize information about reading and writing and answer questions. Invite parents to talk further individually.

Reading Follow-up

Ask parents how their read-alouds at home are going. Encourage questions and sharing of positive stories. Emphasize that reading daily is very important and doesn't need to be done perfectly to be beneficial to children. Model a reading of a book from Unit 3. Address your questions and comments during and after reading to the group, as though reading to a child.

Unit 4

Date:

Dear Family,

We're reading books and talking about colors at school. We hope you'll take some time to notice colors and talk about them at home, too.

The activities on the next page are things you can do to help your child learn. We hope you can complete at least ___ of the activities. Do them in any order. Circle the ones you complete. Then bring the page back to school.

Have fun!

Thank you,

_____

Your child's teacher

Books we are reading at school

- *Max's Dragon Shirt* by Rosemary Wells
- *Dog's Colorful Day* by Emma Dodd
- *The Lion and the Little Red Bird* by Elisa Kleven
- *dear juno* by Soyung Pak
- *Cat's Colors* by Jane Cabrera
- *See How They Grow: Chick* by Jane Burton
- *Chickens Aren't the Only Ones* by Ruth Heller
- *The Tortilla Factory* by Gary Paulsen

Fecha:

Estimada familia,
En la escuela estamos leyendo libros y platicando acerca de los colores. Esperamos que tomen tiempo para observar los colores y también platicar sobre los mismos en su hogar.

Las actividades en la próxima página son cosas que pueden hacer para ayudarle a su hijo/a a aprender. Esperamos que puedan completar por lo menos ___ de las actividades. Las pueden completar en cualquier orden. Circule las que hayan completado. Luego envíen la página de regreso a la escuela.

¡Diviértanse!

Gracias,

_____

El/la maestro/a de su hijo/a

Libros que leemos en inglés en la escuela

- *Max's Dragon Shirt* by Rosemary Wells
- *Dog's Colorful Day* by Emma Dodd
- *The Lion and the Little Red Bird* by Elisa Kleven
- *dear juno* by Soyung Pak
- *Cat´s Colors* by Jane Cabrera
- *See How They Grow: Chick* by Jane Burton
- *Chickens Aren't the Only Ones* by Ruth Heller
- *The Tortilla Factory* by Gary Paulsen

Unit 4
Activities For You And Your Child

Theme of the Month: "Colors."
Thought for the Month: When parents value reading, children do, too.

Read a book. Talk about your child's favorite parts of the story.

As you drive, talk about *uphill*, *downhill*, *under*, *over*, *near*, and *beside*.

Attend a read-aloud at your local library.

Play "Spots!" What would make a purple, brown, or red spot? Your child can look in the cupboard and refrigerator for ideas.

Watch the clock to measure two minutes as you brush your teeth together.

Draw a simple map to show where you live and where school is. Talk about how to get from one place to the other.

Make up easy rhyming riddles for your child to guess: "I'm little and I can crawl or fly. I'm not a rug. I'm not a hug or a mug. I'm a ___ (bug)!"

Cut many small circles, rectangles, and triangles from colorful magazine pages. Use the shapes and a glue stick to make a collage.

At the store, talk about the different departments and what is sold in them. Let your child predict where to find things.

Tell each other what you dreamed last night. Talk about feelings the dreams bring up.

Let your child help open the mail. Talk about what each piece is and show a few words as you read them.

At the grocery store, give color clues for items you plan to buy. Your child can find the rice in the red box or the fruit that's long and yellow.

Write a letter or postcard to a relative. Have your child dictate what to write, then read it aloud.

Let your child tear up lettuce for a salad and name the colors of all the ingredients.

Listen to music. March, bounce, sway, stomp, and clap. Name each action.

Talk about clothes family members are wearing. Find different colors and patterns, like stripes or dots.

Pretend to be birds and fly around. Ask your child what he or she can see in the neighborhood from up in the air.

Turn the tables and let your child "read" a familiar book to you. Talk about it and help if asked, but don't contradict your child's version.

Please return this sheet by _____ . Child_____ Parent _____
                                 (date)   (name)   (name)

Comments? We'd love to hear from you._____

Unidad 4
Actividades para usted y su hijo/a

Nuestro tema del mes es:
"Los colores"

Pensamiento del mes: Cuando los padres valoran la lectura, los niños también harán lo mismo.

Lean un libro. Platiquen sobre las partes que sean las favoritas de su hijo/a.

Mientras maneje, platique sobre *cuesta arriba*, *cuesta abajo*, *por debajo*, *sobre*, *cerca* y *al lado de*.

Asistan a una lectura oral en la biblioteca local.

En la tienda de comestibles, provea pistas de colores para artículos que usted planea comprar. Su hijo/a puede buscar el arroz en la caja roja o la fruta que es larga y amarilla.

Jueguen "¡Manchas!". ¿Qué cosas dejarían una mancha morada, pardo, o roja? Su hijo/a puede mirar en las alacenas o en la refrigeradora por ideas.

Observen el reloj mientras pasan dos minutos de cepillarse los dientes juntos.

Recorte muchos círculos pequeños, rectángulos y triángulos de alguna revista llena de páginas con muchos colores. Usen las diferentes figuras y pegamento para hacer un montaje de recortes.

Dibuje un mapa sencillo del lugar donde viven y la escuela. Platiquen acerca de cómo se llega de un lugar a otro.

Cuéntense el uno al otro lo que soñaron anoche. Platiquen sobre los sentimientos que provocan los sueños.

En la tienda, platique acerca de los diferentes departamentos y lo que cada uno vende. Permita que su hijo/a pueda predecir dónde encontrará ciertos artículos.

Permita que su hijo le ayude abrir la correspondencia. Platique sobre lo que es cada artículo de correspondencia y diga algunas palabras en voz alta mientras las lee.

Pretendan ser pájaros y vuelen. Pregúntele a su hijo/a lo que pueden observar en su vecindario desde arriba en el aire.

Escriban una tarjeta postal o una carta a un familiar. Permita que su hijo dicte lo que se va a escribir, luego léanla en voz alta.

Invente algunas adivinanzas fáciles que rimen y que su hijo/a pueda adivinar: Soy pequeño y puedo arrastrarme o volar. No soy Cleto ni soy Beto. ¡Soy un_____!(insecto).

Escuchen música. Marchen, brinquen, muévanse de un lado al otro, zapateen y aplaudan. Nombren cada acción.

Permita que su hijo desgarre una lechuga para una ensalada y que nombre los colores de todos los ingredientes de la ensalada.

Cambien de papel y permita que su hijo/a le "lea" un libro a usted. Platique sobre el mismo y ayude si su hijo lo pide, pero no contradiga la versión de su hijo.

Platique acerca de la ropa que están vistiendo los miembros de la familia. Señale diferentes colores y patrones, tales como rayas o puntos.

Favor de devolver esta hoja a más tardar _____. _____ del niño/de la niña _____del padre de familia
(fecha)   (nombre)   (nombre)

¿Comentarios? Nos encantaría tener noticias de usted. _____

Unit 4 Workshop: Everyday Letters and Words

This workshop will:
- introduce family members to the content of Unit 4;
- explain the concept of environmental print and the importance of a literacy-rich environment for children;
- provide family members with ideas for using environmental print to support their children's learning.

Suggested Warm-up Activity

Provide pens and paper. Ask parents to list any reading they did today.

Workshop Suggestions

1. Ask parents to share their lists. Create a master list on a flip chart. Add items parents may not have thought of: street signs, traffic signs, ads, menus, bills and mail, house numbers, TV listings, price stickers, size labels, instructions, food labels, calendars, bus identifications, walk/don't walk signs, and so on.

2. Point out that each of these items may provide an opportunity for children to learn about letters, letter sounds, and words. Suggest that environmental print is a perfect way to read and talk about reading every day.

3. Describe a literacy-rich environment. Use examples of print in your classroom to explain how children use environmental print there.

4. Provide specific examples of how families can help children learn using environmental print. Examples might be reading street signs and naming the letters in the words, reading a note aloud, using letter magnets or hand-printed letters on the refrigerator, looking at food boxes and reading some of the words, and so on.

5. Invite questions. Let parents know that you are eager to support their efforts to help their children learn letters and sounds.

To make sure parents know how important they are to their children's learning, give examples of children's comments to you about things they've been doing at home. Instead of using names, say, "One boy said..." and so on.

Be sure parents understand you are not asking them to purchase an array of educational materials. They can help children find print on common things at home and around their neighborhoods.

Unit 4

Introduce the theme of Unit 4: Colors. Give a quick overview of topics, books, and activities. Encourage parents to explore the theme at home as well, noticing and naming colors and playing color games. If there is time, read aloud a book from the unit.

Closing the Workshop

If you haven't already done so, distribute the suggested list of reading books for Units 4 to 6 (page 11). Encourage families to continue reading to their children every day and to point out letters and words around them. Let them know that you invite questions and consider yourself their partner in helping their children learn.

Date:

Dear Family,

We're reading books and talking about shadows and reflections at school. We hope you'll take some time to notice shadows and reflections and talk about them at home, too.

The activities on the next page are things you can do to help your child learn. We hope you can complete at least ___ of the activities. Do them in any order. Circle the ones you complete. Then bring the page back to school.

Have fun!

Thank you,

_____

Your child's teacher

Books we are reading at school

- *Play with Me* by Marie Hall Ets
- *The Puddle Pail* by Elisa Kleven
- *Kitten for a Day* by Ezra Jack Keats
- *Raccoon on His Own* by Jim Arnosky
- *Clap Your Hands* by Lucinda B. Cauley
- *Night Shift Daddy* by Eileen Spinelli
- *Fun With Shadows* by Sharon and Jeff Siamon and Cynthia Benjamin
- *Dreams* by Ezra Jack Keats

Opening the World of Learning™

Fecha:

Estimada familia,

En la escuela estamos leyendo libros acerca de las sombras y los reflejos de luz. Esperamos que ustedes puedan tomar tiempo para observar las sombras y reflejos y también para platicar acerca de esto en su hogar.

Las actividades en la próxima página son cosas que pueden hacer para ayudarle a su hijo/a a aprender. Esperamos que pueda completar por lo menos ___ de las actividades. Las pueden completar en cualquier orden. Circule las que completen. Entonces envíen la página de regreso a la escuela.

¡Diviértanse!

Gracias,

_____

El/la maestro/a de su hijo/a

Libros que leemos en inglés en la escuela

- *Play With Me* by Marie Hall Ets
- *The Puddle Pail* by Elisa Kleven
- *Kitten for a Day* by Ezra Jack Keats
- *Racoon on His Own* by Jim Arnosky
- *Clap Your Hands* by Lucinda B. Cauley
- *Night Shift Daddy* by Eileen Spinelli
- *Fun With Shadows* by Sharon and Jeff Siamon and Cynthia Benjamin
- *Dreams* by Ezra Jack Keats

Unit 5
Activities For You And Your Child

Theme of the Month: "Shadows and Reflections"
Thought for the Month:
Children learn about language through conversations. How much are you talking with your child?

Play *Simon Says*. Use animal movements. Hop like a grasshopper and swim like a fish.

Sit still together and observe birds or other animals. Talk about what you see.

Turn off the lights and play flashlight tag. Use two flashlights, name an object, and see who can hit it first with a flashlight beam.

Sing "Five in a Bed" or another counting song together.

On a sunny day, play with a small mirror indoors. Show how it can reflect light.

Look at a bird book together. Talk about how your favorite birds are alike and how they are different.

Ask your child to help you sort clean laundry. Talk about pairs and how to decide which socks go together.

Have your child hunt for shiny things in your home. Talk about how well you can see your reflections in them.

Tell your child at least three things he or she did well today.

Read a book that you've read before. Let your child say some of the words with you. Give hints by pointing at pictures.

Let your child sort your change. Help him or her name the coins.

Write the numbers 1 to 5 on index cards or paper squares. Make two sets. Turn the cards face down and play a matching game.

On a sunny day, place a plant or other interesting shape on the windowsill. Use paper and a crayon to trace the shadow shape it casts.

Help your child write the letters in his or her name. Talk about how the lines go.

Look in a mirror together and ask your child to describe what he or she sees. Talk about shapes, colors, and how many.

Observe an ant or other insect closely. Talk about what it looks like and what it's doing.

Look at clouds together and talk about the shapes you see.

Find a spider's web and observe it. Then help your child make a web using string and a glue stick.

Please return this sheet by _____ . Child_____ Parent _____
(date)   (name)   (name)

Comments? We'd love to hear from you._____

Unidad 5
Actividades para usted y su hijo/a

Nuestro tema del mes es: "Sombras y reflejos"

Pensamiento del mes: Los niños aprenden el lenguaje a través de conversaciones. ¿Cuánto tiempo pasa usted platicando con su hijo?

Tomen asiento juntos y observen a los pájaros u otros animales. Platiquen acerca de lo que ven.

Un día soleado, jueguen con un espejo dentro de la casa. Muestre cómo refleja la luz.

Jueguen *Simón dice*. Use movimientos de animales. Brinque como un saltamontes y nade como un pez.

Observen juntos las nubes y comenten sobre las formas que ven.

Pídale a su hijo que le ayude a clasificar ropa limpia de la lavada. Platiquen acerca de pares y cómo decidir cuáles calcetines van juntos.

Canten "Cinco elefantes" o cualquier otra canción de contar.

Escriba los números del 1 al 5 en afiches o pedazos de papel cuadrado. Haga dos grupos. Colóquelos boca abajo y jueguen de parear.

Miren juntos un libro sobre aves. Platiquen acerca de cómo sus pájaros favoritos son similares y diferentes.

Apaguen las luces y jueguen de alcanzar y tocar con linternas de bolsillo. Usen dos linternas, nombren un objeto y vean quién es el primero en tocar el objeto con el rayo de luz de la linterna.

Dígale a su hijo/a por lo menos tres cosas que él o ella ha hecho bien hoy.

Haga que su hijo/a busque cosas brillantes en la casa. Platiquen acerca de lo bien que pueden ver su reflejo en ellas.

Permita que su hijo clasifique sus monedas. Ayúdele a nombrar las diferentes monedas.

Observe una hormiga u otro insecto de cerca. Platique acerca de la apariencia y de lo que está haciendo.

Un día soleado, coloque una planta u otra figura interesante sobre el ventanal. Use papel y crayones para trazar la sombra que el objeto produce.

Ayude a su hijo/a a escribir las letras de su nombre. Platique sobre cómo las líneas van en cierta dirección.

Lean un libro que hayan leído anteriormente. Permita que su hijo/a diga algunas de las palabras con usted. Dele pistas, señalando los grabados.

Trate de hallar una telaraña y obsérvenla. Entonces ayúdele a su hijo/a a hacer una telaraña utilizando hilo y pegamento.

Miren juntos en un espejo y pida a su hijo/a que describa lo que él o ella ve. Platiquen acerca de figuras, colores y cantidades.

Favor de devolver esta hoja a más tardar _____. _____ del niño/de la niña _____ del padre de familia

(fecha)   (nombre)   (nombre)

¿Comentarios? Nos encantaría tener noticias de usted. _____

Unit 5 Workshop: Math Every Day

This workshop will:
- introduce family members to the content of Unit 5;
- identify basic math concepts and activities children are learning at school;
- provide family members with ideas for supporting development of math concepts and skills at home.

Suggested Warm-up Activity

Choose a math activity from Unit 5 for parents to complete. One possibility is "Making Collections," on pages 55–56 of the teacher's guide. Have the materials and record sheet ready to use when parents arrive.

Workshop Suggestions

1. Talk about the Warm-up. List the math skills involved in the activity. Invite parents to identify how each skill was applied.

2. Explain that math involves not only counting, but sorting things into categories, learning to recognize shapes and sizes, and understanding spatial relations, such as *on top*, *under*, and *beside*. Emphasize the idea that the more experiences in math-related activities children have at this age, the more prepared they will be to understand math in school.

3. Present ways parents can help children learn at home:
   - helping them count the number of people for dinner
   - guessing how many spoonfuls of cereal are left in the bowl and counting as they eat them
   - naming shapes of traffic signs, patterns on rugs, and so on
   - pointing out stripes and other patterns
   - comparing sizes of shoes or socks
   - helping them measure using string

4. Invite questions. Let parents know that encouraging their children in ordinary math experiences daily at home will support your efforts in school.

Keep in Mind...
Make sure parents know they can support math concepts at home through everyday, concrete experiences and exploration, rather than math drills.

Unit 5

Introduce the theme of Unit 5: Shadows and Reflections. Quickly review topics, books, and activities. If there is time, read a book from the unit. Encourage parents to explore the theme at home as well, talking about reflections in shiny surfaces and observing and describing shadows.

Present home math ideas that are simple and easy to do. Do not expect parents to purchase special materials.

Closing the Workshop

Distribute "Math at Home" (pages 12–15). Let parents know that they can come to you with questions.

Date:

Dear Family,

At school, we're reading books and talking about things that grow, like plants, animals, and people, too! We hope you'll take some time to talk about growing things at home as well.

The activities on the next page are things you can do to help your child learn. We hope you can complete at least ___ of the activities. Do them in any order. Circle the ones you complete. Then bring the page back to school.

Have fun!

Thank you,

_____

Your child's teacher

Books we are reading at school

- *The Ugly Vegetables* by Grace Lin
- *Make Way for Ducklings* by Robert McCloskey
- *I Heard Said the Bird* by Polly Berends
- *Bigger* by Daniel Kirk
- *Just Enough* by Teri Daniels
- *See How They Grow: Duck* by Jane Burton
- *Growing Things* by Dawn Sirett and Lara Tankel
- *Animals Born Alive* and *Well* by Ruth Heller

Opening the World of Learning™

Fecha:

Estimada familia,

En la escuela estamos leyendo libros y platicando acerca de las cosas que crecen, tales como las plantas, los animales, y ¡también la gente! Esperamos que ustedes también puedan tomar tiempo para platicar en su hogar sobre cosas que crecen.

Las actividades en la siguiente página son cosas que pueden hacer para ayudarle a su hijo/a a aprender. Esperamos que puedan completar por lo menos ___ de las actividades. Las pueden completar en cualquier orden. Circule las que hayan completado. Luego envíen la página de regreso a la escuela.

¡Diviértanse!

Gracias,

_____

El/la maestro/a de su hijo/a

Libros que leemos en inglés en la escuela

- *The Ugly Vegetables* by Grace Lin
- *Make Way for Ducklings* by Robert McCloskey
- *I Heard Said the Bird* by Polly Berends
- *Bigger* by Daniel Kirk
- *Just Enough* by Teri Daniels
- *See How They Grow: Duck* by Jane Burton
- *Growing Things* by Dawn Sirett and Lara Tankel
- *Animals Born Alive and Well* by Ruth Heller

Unit 6
Activities For You And Your Child

Theme of the Month: "Things That Grow"

Thought for the Month: Children who have a caring adult who reads to them and talks with them, every day, do better in school.

Close your eyes and stay still. Talk with your child about the sounds you both hear.

Talk about three things your child can do now that he or she couldn't do when younger.

Write a note thanking your child for helping today. Read it aloud, then display it in your child's room.

Ask your child to teach you a song he or she learned at school.

Have soup for lunch. Identify the ingredients and talk about vegetables.

Look at a rack of seed packets at the store. Talk about the pictures and read and spell out some of the plant names.

Exercise to music with your child. Have fun and talk about bending, stretching, and twisting.

Take a walk together. Talk about the rules for crossing the street.

Put a plant cutting in water in a clear bottle. Watch as roots sprout and talk about how plants grow.

Let your child choose a favorite soup at the grocery store. Talk about the picture and read some of the words on the can.

Talk about something you learned to do as a child. Explain how you felt when you were trying and when you finally could do it.

Place a small surprise somewhere. Then use directions to get your child to it: "Take 3 steps, Turn left. Bend down. Look under something."

Ask a neighbor to show you his or her garden. Talk about the sights and smells.

Read a storybook. During the story, talk about why the characters act as they do.

Go for a walk together. Observe big things and little things, things that grow and things that do not grow.

Help your child measure a room or hallway by counting how many steps from one side to the other.

Sprout alfalfa seeds between clean, damp paper towels. Observe and talk about how they grew. Then eat them on a salad.

Please return this sheet by _____. Child_____ Parent _____
                         (date)   (name)   (name)

Comments? We'd love to hear from you._____

_____

Unit 6
Actividades Para Usted y Su Hijo/a

Nuestro tema del mes es: "Cosas que crecen"

Pensamiento del mes: Los niños que tienen adultos que se preocupan por ellos, que les lee y platica cada día, les va mejor en la escuela.

Platique con su hijo/a acerca de tres cosas que puede hacer ahora y que no podía hacer cuando era más joven.

Haga brotar semillas de alfalfa entre toallas limpias y húmedas. Observe y platique acerca de cómo crecen. Luego coma la alfalfa en una ensalada.

Haga ejercicios acompañado/a de música con su hijo/a. Diviértanse y platiquen acerca de doblarse, estirarse y virarse.

Pídale a su hijo/a que le enseñe a cantar una canción que aprendió en la escuela.

Caminen juntos. Platiquen sobre las reglas de "cruce de calle".

Tomen sopa a la hora de almuerzo. Identifiquen los ingredientes y platiquen sobre los vegetales.

Observe semillas en paquetes en una tienda. Platique acerca de las ilustraciones y lea y deletree algunos de los nombres de las plantas.

Platique acerca de algo que aprendió a hacer de niño/a. Explique cómo se sentía cuando lo intentaba y cuando finalmente lo logró.

Coloque una sorpresita en algún lugar. Entonces dé instrucciones para que su hijo/a la encuentre: "Toma tres pasos, gira hacia la izquierda, agáchate. Busca debajo algo".

Pida a un vecino que les muestre su patio o jardín. Platiquen acerca de cosas que ven y olores que perciben.

Coloque un corte de una planta en agua dentro un envase transparente. Observen cómo las raíces brotan y platiquen acerca de cómo crecen las plantas.

Permita que su hijo/a escoja una sopa favorita en la tienda de comestibles. Platique sobre la ilustración y lea algunas de las palabras en el enlatado.

Ayúdele a su hijo/a a medir una habitación o pasillo contando los pasos de un lado al otro.

Cierren los ojos y permanezcan quietos. Platique con su hijo/a acerca de los sonidos que escuchan juntos.

Escriba una nota agradeciéndole a su hijo/a por ayudarle hoy. Léala en voz alta, luego exhíbala en la habitación de su hijo/a.

Lea un libro de cuentos. Durante la lectura del cuento, platique sobre la razón de las acciones de los personajes.

Tomen juntos una caminata. Observen cosas grandes y cosas pequeñas, cosas que crecen y cosas que no crecen.

Favor de devolver esta hoja a más tardar _____. _____ del niño/de la niña _____ del padre de familia
(fecha)   (nombre)   (nombre)

¿Comentarios? Nos encantaría tener noticias de usted. _____

Unit 6 Workshop: Your Growing Child

This workshop will:
- introduce family members to the content of Unit 6;
- identify social and emotional skills that preschoolers are developing;
- explain ways social-emotional development is fostered in your classroom.

Suggested Warm-up Activity

Ask family members to think about a time in the last few weeks when they needed to ask their child to wait or to share. Compile a list of common situations.

Workshop Suggestions

1. Discuss the strong emotions that often come up when young children anticipate events or don't want to share.

2. Point out that social and emotional skills must be learned and practiced, just like any other new skills. Share examples from your classroom that show how children have grown in this area during the year. Examples might include the following:
   - waiting for a turn to talk during Story Time
   - sharing a can of markers at the writing center
   - dividing vehicles among children in the blocks play area
   - not crying when they don't get a first turn
   - waiting patiently in line without pushing

3. Explain your expectations for children's behavior in the areas of patience and a willingness to take turns; empathy and tolerance for others; self-control and dealing with emotions; sharing; and cooperation.

4. Share strategies you use to foster children's social and emotional growth. Emphasize the importance of a) classroom routines and rules in helping children develop trust and patience; and b) helping children acquire the words they need to use in emotionally charged situations.

> **Keep in Mind...**
> Share your expectations for children's behavior in your classroom and explain how you foster social and emotional growth, while avoiding giving parenting advice.

Unit 6

Introduce the theme of Unit 6: Things That Grow. Give a quick overview of topics, books, and activities. Encourage parents to help children explore the theme at home as well, observing growing things around them and their own physical and developmental growth.

> Encourage parents to continue to read, talk, and do informal math activities with their children every day. Let them know that you are happy to answer questions.

Closing the Workshop

Read aloud the poem "I Have No Trouble Sharing" by Robert Scotellaro (from *A Bad Case of the Giggles*, selected by Bruce Lansky, New York: Meadowbrook Press, 1994). Remind parents to keep their sense of humor as their children learn social skills.

Date:

Dear Parent or Caregiver:

Believe it or not, kindergarten is just around the corner!

Over the summer, you can continue to prepare your child for the big day. Read to your child as often as you can. Talk about kindergarten, what it will be like, and your child's feelings about the change. (Talk to your child about lots of other things, too!) You may want to schedule a tour of the school, so both you and your child will feel more comfortable with the change.

In kindergarten, the teacher will expect children to be able to do these things:

- hold a pencil for writing
- follow rules and directions
- take turns
- listen to a story in a group
- work independently sometimes
- go to the toilet and wash hands

If you have questions about how to sign up for kindergarten or what you need to do to prepare (doctor's exam, and so on) please call
_____ at _____.

It's been a great year. I wish you and your child all the best.

_____

Your child's teacher

Fecha:

Estimado padre de familia o encargado:
Aunque no lo crea, ¡kindergarten está a la vuelta de la esquina! (se aproxima).

Durante el verano, usted puede continuar preparando a su hijo/a para el gran día. Léale a su hijo/a cuantas veces pueda. Platique con él/ella acerca del kindergarten, cómo será, y de lo que siente él/ella acerca del cambio que se avecina. (¡Platique también con su hijo/a acerca de muchas otras cosas!) Talvez usted desee programar un recorrido de la escuela, para que ambos puedan sentirse más cómodos con el cambio.

En kindergarten, la maestra espera que los niños sepan hacer lo siguiente:

- Sostener un lápiz para escribir
- Seguir reglas e instrucciones
- Tomar turnos
- Escuchar un cuento en grupo
- Trabajar independientemente de vez en cuando
- Ir al baño y lavarse las manos

Si tiene alguna pregunta acerca del proceso de matrícula para kindergarten o lo que necesita preparar (examen del doctor, etc.) favor de llamar a
_____ al _____.

Ha sido un año fantástico. Le deseo a usted y su hijo lo mejor.

_____

El/la maestro/a de su hijo/a

Dear Parents and Caregivers,

Please join us for a workshop!

Date: _____   Time: _____

Place: _____

Topic: _____

During this workshop, we will share what we're busy doing in the classroom. We'll also provide suggestions for helping your child learn at home.

I hope very much to see you there!

_____

Your child's teacher

- -

Invitación a talleres

Estimados padres de familia y encargados,
¡Los invitamos a participar en un taller con nosotros!

Fecha: _____   Hora: _____

Lugar: _____

Tema: _____

Durante el taller, les contaremos lo que hacemos en el salón de clases.

También brindaremos sugerencias para ayudarle a su hijo/a a aprender en casa.

¡Espero verlos ahí!

_____

El/la maestro/a de su hijo/a